BOO BOO STEWART

GET THE SCOOP

the

HOTTEST
WEREWOLF
IN-TRAINING

NEW KID
ON THE
BLOCK

nauthorized
iography
y Sean Thomas

TEAM
Boo Boo

PSS!
PRICE STERN SLOAN
An Imprint of Penguin Group (USA) Inc.

PRICE STERN SLOAN
Published by the Penguin Group
Penguin Group (USA) Inc., 375 Hudson Street, New York, New York 10014, USA
Penguin Group (Canada), 90 Eglinton Avenue East, Suite 700,
Toronto, Ontario M4P 2Y3, Canada
(a division of Pearson Penguin Canada Inc.)
Penguin Books Ltd., 80 Strand, London WC2R 0RL, England
Penguin Group Ireland, 25 St. Stephen's Green, Dublin 2, Ireland
(a division of Penguin Books Ltd.)
Penguin Group (Australia), 250 Camberwell Road, Camberwell, Victoria 3124, Australia
(a division of Pearson Australia Group Pty. Ltd.)
Penguin Books India Pvt. Ltd., 11 Community Centre, Panchsheel Park,
New Delhi—110 017, India
Penguin Group (NZ), 67 Apollo Drive, Rosedale, North Shore 0632, New Zealand
(a division of Pearson New Zealand Ltd.)
Penguin Books (South Africa) (Pty.) Ltd., 24 Sturdee Avenue,
Rosebank, Johannesburg 2196, South Africa

Penguin Books Ltd., Registered Offices: 80 Strand, London WC2R 0RL, England

Photo credits: Cover: Photo by Eric Shimohata; Insert photos: first page courtesy of Eric
Shimohata/PR Photos; second page courtesy of Michael Buckner/Getty Images; Photo by
Kevin Winter/Getty Images; third page courtesy of Frazer Harrison/Getty Images;
Michael Tran/FilmMagic; fourth page courtesy of Jordan Strauss/Getty Images.

Library of Congress Control Number: 2010002408

ISBN 978-0-8431-9900-0   10 9 8 7 6 5 4 3 2 1

CONTENTS

Introduction   5

Chapter 1   Baby Boo Boo   9

Chapter 2   The Real Karate Kid   19

Chapter 3   Boo Boo's Big Break   27

Chapter 4   Boo Boo Hits the Big Screen!   43

Chapter 5   Hi-Ho, Hi-Ho, It's Off to Disney Boo Boo Goes! 51

Chapter 6   T-Squad Powers, Activate!   61

Chapter 7   The Search for Seth Clearwater   73

Chapter 8   Eclipse Rising   87

Chapter 9   What's Next for Boo Boo?   95

Chapter 10   Boo Boo and His Fans   101

Chapter 11   Fun, Fast Boo Boo Facts   109

Chapter 12   How Well Do You Know Boo Boo?   113

Chapter 13   What Kind of Boo Boo Fan Are You?   121

Chapter 14   Boo Boo Online   125

INTRODUCTION

Halloween is one of the most fun holidays of the year. It's when everyone—kids *and* adults—dress up in outrageous costumes and pretend to be other people for a day. This applies to actors and actresses, too. Even though actors spend their days pretending to be other people on movie and television sets, they must still love to put on a costume and transform into somebody different.

In October 2009, Boo Boo Stewart knew exactly who he wanted to dress up as for Halloween: the superhero Batman's creepy arch-nemesis, the Joker. Before the big day, Boo Boo talked to *Popstar!* magazine about what he wanted to be for Halloween: "Heath Ledger's Joker [from the 2008 movie *The Dark Knight*]. That's such an amazing movie, and the character is awesome!" Boo Boo liked the movie so much that he even bought and was photographed wearing a T-shirt with the late actor Heath Ledger's version of the character on it. Showing off his fandom on a T-shirt was great, but this was Boo Boo's chance to actually become the character in real life!

In the days leading up to October 31, Boo Boo posted updates for his fans on Twitter. He told them that he was working on his costume, and that it was turning out to be "so cool." Like any other fifteen-year-old kid out to have a good time on Halloween, Boo Boo obviously wanted his costume to look as amazing—and realistic—as possible. And all that hard work paid off. Boo Boo made a really convincing Joker! On October 31, when Boo Boo put on his costume, teased his normally shiny, healthy brown hair into the Joker's signature scraggly look, and painted his face with pale white makeup and a creepy red smile, he had to be amazed at what he saw. He looked just like the Joker, in the role that won Heath Ledger an Academy Award for Best Supporting Actor!

But at the time Boo Boo probably didn't even think about the most *amazing* thing: Next Halloween, he might not be the one dressing up in costume as someone else—his fans might be dressing up as him! Because by then, Boo Boo would be known to audiences around the world as Seth Clearwater, the latest addition to the cast of superhot superstars in *Eclipse*, the third movie in The Twilight Saga, which is based on a book of the same name in the popular *Twilight* series by Stephenie Meyer.

Though at the time Boo Boo *did* know that his fans were super excited about him playing the character of Seth, one of the youngest members of the La Push pack of werewolves. In fact, before the third movie was cast, some of his fans had even posted homemade videos on YouTube, suggesting Boo Boo as the perfect actor for the part. That was before he even auditioned for the role! And so it must have been pretty amazing for Boo Boo to realize that the following Halloween, he might catch a glimpse of his own fans walking around dressed like their favorite new *Twilight* character, Seth Clearwater! And how cool would that be?

CHAPTER 1

BABY BOO BOO

Twilight fans might know him as Boo Boo, but when he was born on January 21, 1994, the talented actor, singer, dancer, and martial artist was actually named Nils Allen Stewart Jr. after his father. Boo Boo's parents, Nils Allen Stewart Sr. and Renee Stewart, were incredibly excited when their little boy was born. At the time of Boo Boo's birth, the Stewart family, including Boo Boo's older sister, Maegan, who was born in 1987, lived in Beverly Hills, California—the real-life location of the popular CW television show *90210*!

It was probably destiny that little baby Nils would grow up to become Boo Boo the movie star, since Beverly Hills is home to countless movie stars and Hollywood celebrities. Beverly Hills is located in the western part of Los Angeles, California. It is known for glamorous shopping areas like Rodeo Drive, and world-famous places like Sunset Boulevard, which has been immortalized in many movies and television shows—in fact, the classic movie *Sunset Boulevard*, about an aging actress, Norma Desmond, was so revered that it was turned into a Broadway musical of the same name!

In addition to the original FOX network television show *Beverly Hills, 90210*, which ran from 1990 to 2000, and the latest version, *90210*, which currently airs on the CW, the area has also been glamorously depicted in movies like *Beverly Hills Chihuahua*, and even in the song "Beverly Hills" by the rock band Weezer. There was even a sitcom on CBS back in the '60s called *The Beverly Hillbillies*, which now appears in reruns on TV Land. It was about a backwoods family from Texas who struck oil and used their newfound riches to move to Beverly Hills, even though they were more comfortable living the "simple life" back home in Texas!

It's no accident that the Stewarts lived in Beverly Hills—Nils Allen Stewart Sr. has been working in Hollywood since before Boo Boo was even born! Nils Sr. started working as an actor and stuntman in movies almost twenty years ago. Since then he has acted in popular movies like the 1994 comedy smash *The Mask* (starring Jim Carrey and Cameron Diaz), director Tim Burton's inventive 2001 reimagining of the 1968 sci-fi classic *Planet of the Apes* (starring Mark Wahlberg and Helena Bonham Carter), and *The Scorpion King*, the 2002 sequel to 2001's *The Mummy Returns*, starring Dwayne "The Rock" Johnson. Nils Sr. has also appeared in episodes of TV series like *Charmed* (1998–2006), about the Halliwell sisters (played by Shannen Doherty, Holly Marie Combs, Alyssa Milano, and later Rose McGowan) who discover they are witches, and the long-running medical drama *ER* (1994–2009), about an emergency room (or ER) at the fictional County General Hospital in Chicago—the same television show where Boo Boo would also make a guest appearance years later!

In addition, Nils Sr.'s accomplished stunt work can be seen in exciting, action-filled movies like *Charlie's Angels* (based on the classic 1970s ABC television show, the 2000 box office smash starred Cameron Diaz, Drew Barrymore, and Lucy Liu), the superhero flick *Daredevil* (which was released in 2003, and starred Ben Affleck, Jennifer Garner, and Colin Farrell), and 2006's *Eragon*, based on the successful children's book series by Christopher Paolini about a boy who hatches a dragon from an egg. It seems that Nils Jr. *and* Sr. know how to use their fighting moves to land parts in exciting action movies. It also seems like acting and stunt work were professions Boo Boo was born to do!

Nils Sr. and his wife, Renee, must have been the proudest of parents when their little, brown-eyed baby boy was born. Boo Boo's January birthday means that he was born under the astrological sign of the zodiac known as Aquarius. Some people believe that, based on the position of the planets when you were born, your horoscope can help to determine your path in life. Aquarius is the eleventh of the twelve signs of the zodiac. Most Aquarians, like Boo Boo, are considered to be adaptable and outgoing individuals who are very original and like to take chances. They are also considered very honest and loyal friends. That sure sounds like Boo Boo!

However, because Boo Boo was born on the first day of the sign of Aquarius, he's a bit unique. (Like we didn't already know that!) Aquarians born on January 21 can appear to be cool and collected on the outside, but they still have a certain magnetism that draws the spotlight to them. They are usually intelligent, but with a great sense of humor, even about themselves. They can also be perfectionists when it comes to how they approach their work. That could help to explain why Boo Boo is so good at everything he does!

When Boo Boo's parents brought their new baby boy home to his sister Maegan, who was six years old at the time, they decided to name him Nils Jr., after his father. Nils is traditionally a Swedish or Norwegian variation of the name Nicholas. The original Greek meaning of the name Nicholas is "victory of the people." Saint Nicholas was a bishop who lived back in the fourth century, and is remembered as the patron saint of children, sailors, and merchants. One of the most famous Nicholases in the world is Saint Nick, or Santa Claus!

Boo Boo's last name, Stewart, also has a meaning. In western countries like the United States, family names or surnames are also known as last names.

But in some eastern countries, such as China, Japan, Korea, and Vietnam, the family name comes first! The roots of many common last names, or surnames, can be traced back to their roots as occupations of ancestors who held those jobs. Stewart is one such occupational name. It is based on the occupation of a steward, who was the person who managed an important person's household or estate. So one loose interpretation of the name Nils Stewart would be "of the people and for the people."

But, as time would tell, Nils Jr. wouldn't be the name to stick to the energetic baby boy the Stewarts brought into the world in 1994. It seems a habit little Nils had as a baby led to him getting his nickname Boo Boo! "When I was a baby, I always used to suck my two fingers and my parents said I had a boo-boo face, so that's how I got my name," Boo Boo told kidzworld.com. How cute—and how lucky for the rising star that his parents gave him such an unusual nickname that everyone would be sure to remember!

Boo Boo owes his gorgeous looks in part to his very unique heritage, which he got from his parents. His mother Renee's lineage is Japanese, Chinese, and

Korean, while his father Nils's lineage is Scottish, Russian, and Blackfoot Indian. Talk about an eclectic family tree! Boo Boo's unique looks have helped him land some awesome roles because they allow him to play lots of different types of nationalities. And Boo Boo wasn't the only Stewart kid blessed with these good looks! In addition to his older sister, Maegan, born in 1987, Boo Boo also has two younger sisters: Trent Heaven, born in 1996, who, like Boo Boo, one day decided that she would prefer to go by a nickname, Fivel, instead of her given name; and Sage, who was born in 2005, which makes her the youngest of the Stewart clan. And all of the Stewarts are growing up to be quite talented, with aspirations in show business, just like their dad. Nils Sr. and Renee must be incredibly proud of all of them!

But just like any other family with lots of kids, the Stewarts have to put a little work into getting along—especially when it comes to sharing the bathroom! The Stewart family home only has one bathroom for all the kids to share, and with his sisters often vying for time in front of the mirror, Boo Boo frequently has to wait a while for his turn! It seems that the bathroom policy in the Stewart household is first come, first served. Good to know! "Oh man, I love my sisters, but this thing they have with camping out in the bathroom, I can't even explain it," Boo Boo told *Lunchbox* magazine. "If I don't somehow get in there first, I might as well forget ever seeing it at all. They will stay in there for at least an hour, and no amount of begging on my part is going to move them out until they think they are done." Poor Boo Boo must sometimes feel like he's getting ganged up on, being the only boy in a house full of sisters! Sounds like even though he's a movie star, Boo Boo still has to deal with some of the same problems lots of brothers have with their sisters. But no matter how often they may bicker, Boo Boo and his sisters are still very close. Boo Boo is especially close to his sis Fivel. Not only do they genuinely enjoy hanging out together, they also enjoy performing music together, and shooting videos—which they will often upload to YouTube for their fans to watch. Boo Boo even brought Fivel along as his date to the premiere of *New Moon*! Talk about an awesome big brother!

They might get on one another's nerves

sometimes, just like a lot of siblings do, but all of the Stewart kids seem to get along—and that's a good thing, especially for a family that spends as much time together as the Stewarts do. Boo Boo and his sisters don't go to a regular public or private school with other students. Their parents are in charge of educating them through homeschooling, so that they can have a flexible schedule for whatever acting projects they are working on. This is a common thing for actors and kids living in Hollywood, but it means that the Stewarts are together a lot more often than most families. But it seems like Boo Boo doesn't mind! On his Twitter page, Boo Boo tweeted to his fans, "I am homeschooled and love it." It also doesn't hurt that Boo Boo is a good student. No matter what acting project he's working on at the moment, he still makes time to study so that he can maintain his grades—straight As!

Boo Boo is also proud of his membership in a Gifted and Talented Education (GATE) program for academically gifted children. The purpose of GATE programs is to seek out students with exceptional abilities, so that they can have opportunities for enriched and challenging educations. Students are usually selected for GATE programs based on their aptitude for giftedness in the areas of original thought, prediction, planning, decision making, social expressions, and learning and academics. Sounds pretty awesome. No wonder Boo Boo is proud of being selected—and we're sure his parents are very proud of him, too!

CHAPTER 2
THE REAL KARATE KID

Boo Boo hasn't been a martial artist since the day he was born—but based on all the martial arts and stunt work he would go on to do in his career, it sure seems that way! Though Boo Boo did first start learning karate when he was just a little boy. "I've done karate since I was three, and was always around stunts my whole life," Boo Boo told *Inspire* magazine. He was obviously dedicated to the sport from a very young age, which must have been how he got to be so good at it. As the old saying goes: Practice makes perfect!

In fact, Boo Boo got so good at martial arts that only five years later, in 2002, he was named Martial Arts World Champion for his division! And to top it off, he won the title again in 2003! The next year, Boo Boo was inducted into the 2004 Martial Arts Junior Hall of Fame, and he was only ten years old! That's quite an accomplishment!

But being inducted into the Martial Arts Junior Hall of Fame didn't mean that Boo Boo was finished with his martial arts training—far from it! Little did he know at the time, but Boo Boo was about to follow in the footsteps of his future *Eclipse* costar and fellow werewolf Taylor Lautner! It seems that just like Taylor, Boo Boo was looking to explore the next level of his martial arts expertise, and wanted to be able to combine his athletic skills with his goal of becoming an action star. And that led him to the Xtreme Martial Arts Performance Training Program.

Headquartered in North Hollywood, California, just a few blocks away from the famous Universal Studios movie lot, Xtreme Martial Arts (or, as its fans call it, XMA) was developed by superstar martial artist Mike Chat. Mike Chat is known as the Tony Hawk of the martial arts world—he's a seven-time World Forms and Weapons Champion, and was inducted into the World Martial Arts Hall of Fame in 1992. He is also an accomplished stuntman and actor who starred as a member of one of the most iconic groups of martial arts heroes of all time—

the Blue Power Ranger, Chad Lee, on the popular television series *Power Rangers Lightspeed Rescue!*

In 1998, Mike started an elite level training camp at the University of California–Los Angeles, better known as UCLA. Together with his future wife, McKenzie Satterthwaite, they developed XMA over a three-year period, turning it into an exciting series of innovative and revolutionary training programs that are now used in over seven hundred martial arts schools worldwide. The XMA Performance Training Program uses martial arts as a tool to develop life and leadership skills.

As for the martial arts aspect of XMA, Mike decided that he wanted to incorporate as many different elements of performance into the XMA style of martial arts as possible. Mike had a strong background in Tae Kwon Do and kickboxing, as well as yoga, ballet, and acrobatics, and he wanted to create a style of training that would help his students master the kind of martial artistry seen in video games and Hollywood movies. "That's what everyone sees—in TV, on the video games that they play, in *Power Rangers*—and so we just put it into a program so now people can learn how to do it," Mike told younghollywood.com. "When you see [*The*] *Matrix*, and you go to martial arts school, now you can get *Matrix* moves, not just *Karate Kid*."

The exciting new XMA style quickly became popular with many karate students who were looking to develop their skills in an edgy, thrilling way. Among those students was a young Taylor Lautner! Taylor took to this exciting new style of martial arts right away. By the end of his first XMA summer camp, Taylor was doing cartwheels with no hands! XMA soon began to attract lots of fans in the entertainment industry, and even musical megastars like R&B singer Usher and Black Eyed Peas member Apl.de.ap. were clamoring to work with XMA to help develop hot new action-based choreography for their performances.

Considering XMA's popularity and rigorous training program, it's no surprise that someone as ambitious as Boo Boo would decide to get involved with the program. Another not-so-surprising thing: He was a natural! "It's really cool," Boo Boo told younghollywood.com. Thanks to his time at XMA,

Boo Boo learned lots of new moves that he couldn't wait to try out. "I love the trampoline. I'll do a round-off layout and I'll just, like, hold it . . . and it just feels like flying!" After seeing Boo Boo in action, younghollywood.com was so impressed with Boo Boo and his moves that they called him "the real Karate Kid"—and who can blame them?

Boo Boo's excitement over his XMA training must have been contagious, because soon his little sister Fivel was training at the headquarters, too! But Fivel is an accomplished martial artist in her own right. Just like Boo Boo, she started karate at a young age: five years old. The next year, at only six years old, she started competing, and just like her older brother, Boo Boo, Fivel also won the 2002 and 2003 World Championships in Martial Arts! And in 2003, she was inducted into the Black Belt Junior Hall of Fame! Fivel also loves gymnastics and dance, and has won dance scholarships at every competition she has entered. No wonder the two of them are such good friends, in addition to being brother and sister—they have so much in common!

But as much as Boo Boo enjoyed his time

training at XMA, he didn't want to limit his martial arts development to just that one area. That's why he jumped at the chance to join another martial arts group! In October 2004, a junior version of the popular Sideswipe performance group was created, called the Sideswipe Kids—and Boo Boo was asked to join! Sideswipe is known for combining music and acrobatic choreography with extreme martial arts moves to create unique, exciting performances. Five-time world martial arts champ Matt Mullins handpicks everyone who performs with the Sideswipe crews, and he personally asked Boo Boo to join the Sideswipe Kids. What an honor!

One of Sideswipe's goals is to promote a positive image of honesty and integrity through martial arts. Members are selected not only based on their skill level, but also on their integrity, energy, and work ethic. With those qualities, it makes sense that Boo Boo would be a perfect fit for the group. He definitely had the necessary work ethic: Boo Boo dedicated himself to learning and mastering his martial arts moves at a very young age. And he always tried to encourage others to do their best, too.

Boo Boo shared this positive advice for his fans with *Teen Scene* magazine: "Never quit. And practice practice practice."

Boo Boo worked really hard, and had an easy time fitting in with the rest of the Sideswipe crew. One of the highlights? In February 2005, Boo Boo and the rest of the Sideswipe Kids made their first national televised performance on *The Ellen DeGeneres Show*! Wearing navy karate pants and bright red T-shirts, and taking the stage to the classic dance anthem "Gonna Make You Sweat (Everybody Dance Now)" by C+C Music Factory, Boo Boo and the rest of the team were soon kicking and flipping all over the stage! The audience cheered and screamed with applause, and even Ellen herself said, "How amazing are they?!" Pretty amazing, indeed! In fact, their performance was highlighted in the May 2005 issue of *Tae Kwon Do Times*!

Also in February 2005, the Sideswipe Kids, including Boo Boo, held a performance weekend that featured thirty performers from all over the country who flew in just to participate. The kids performed a cool, futuristic routine with the stage bathed in black light, so only their hats, gloves, shoes, and weapons like nunchuks and bolos were visible to the audience. They also did fun routines based on the *Star Wars* movies and the cartoon *The Powerpuff Girls*! Audiences were surely wowed by the displays. With talent like that, it was only a matter of time before Boo Boo was able to put his stellar martial arts and performing skills to use in Hollywood!

CHAPTER 3
BOO BOO'S BIG BREAK

Today, Boo Boo is a successful actor with a growing résumé and has a talent agent who helps him find and secure the roles he decides to pursue. Boo Boo is signed to Matthew Jackson of the Jackson Agency in Los Angeles, California. Matt has been called one of the best acting coaches for kids, and has specialized in youth projects for TV and movies for over a dozen years. And he obviously knows his stuff—Matt formerly worked as the director of talent development for the Disney Channel, where he helped to develop the careers of young performers like Shia LaBeouf and Hilary Duff! So Boo Boo's career is obviously in good hands. But his first exposure to show business was much closer to home—in fact, it was right at home!

Since his dad was an actor and stuntman in Hollywood movies and television shows, little Boo Boo had grown up exposed to the entertainment industry basically since the time he was born. At the time of Boo Boo's birth, Nils Sr. probably didn't know what kind of impact his career would have on his son. Nevertheless, it seems like Boo Boo—and his sisters—couldn't wait to follow their dad into the family business: show business!

Boo Boo has always looked up to his father, and like a lot of little boys, probably wanted to grow up and be just like him. "My dad was a stunt coordinator," Boo Boo told *Kidsday*. "He has been in the business since I was born. I just decided I wanted to be in the business, and I started acting." And it was his dad who helped to open that first door into the entertainment industry for Boo Boo. Not surprising, because Boo Boo's first role was in a movie that Nils Sr. and Boo Boo's older sister, Maegan, were already working on!

Maegan, like Boo Boo, got her first taste of acting at an early age. In 1996, when she was only nine years old, she was cast in the role of a kidnapped little girl in an action movie that Nils Sr. was working on as a stunt coordinator called *Warrior of Justice*. The movie, which was also known as *Invitation to*

Die when it was released on home video, was about martial artists who must fight to the death. Even though Maegan didn't receive an on-screen credit for her part in the movie, that didn't deter her!

The next year, Maegan got a part in another project her father was working on, a TV movie called *Mercenary*, starring John Ritter (*Three's Company, 8 Simple Rules . . . for Dating My Teenage Daughter*) as a rich businessman whose wife is killed by kidnappers. Nils Sr. played the role of Bad Dave, and while Maegan was yet again not credited for playing a child in the movie, it was another taste of what it was like to work in the industry. She and her father also worked as animal wranglers on the movie. She took a few years off, but then in 2004, she and her dad signed on to do a movie called *Skeleton Man*, the same movie younger brother Boo Boo would also get the chance to work on!

"My dad and my older sister Maegan were doing a movie called *Skeleton Man*," Boo Boo told *Teen Scene* magazine. "They needed a Native American kid so they hired me." Boo Boo, who was only ten years old when *Skeleton Man* was released in 2004, was cast as an extra, which is a non-speaking role in a film. He played the role of Child Warrior, while Maegan played the role of Indian Princess. Nils Sr. played the role of Sergeant Rodriguez, and all three of them also contributed to the stunt work in the film. The made-for-television movie was a thriller about a mysterious supernatural being who was awakened when scientists disturbed its Native American burial ground.

Boo Boo might not have had a large role in the movie, but it was definitely enough to whet his appetite for the movie business! Boo Boo quickly went looking for more work. That same year, Boo Boo and little sis Fivel both appeared in bit roles in an independent movie called *Yard Sale*, about a divorcing couple who decide to sell off their possessions at a yard sale so they can split the profits and go their separate ways. Boo Boo was credited in the role of Little Boy, and Fivel played the role of Chrissy Deavers, but unfortunately, the movie was not picked up for distribution in theaters or on video and was only screened at film festivals.

One year later, Boo Boo and Fivel were at it

again when they signed on to do stunts for a 2005 made-for-TV documentary special that their father was working on, called *The Kings of Babylon*, about the history of Iraq. It was another great experience, and only made young Boo Boo anxious to get more work. So it must have been super-exciting when Boo Boo and his sisters Maegan and Fivel all appeared together in a martial arts action movie called *Pit Fighter*. The movie, which was released on DVD in 2005, is about a man named Jack (played by Dominiquie Vandenberg) who cannot remember anything except how to fight.

It was really fun for eleven-year-old Boo Boo to work on major movie sets as an extra and a stunt double. He was soaking up experiences that some actors twice his age only dream of! But young Boo Boo had bigger dreams than that. That's why he was probably ecstatic when, that same year, he got what was arguably his first big break. Boo Boo was chosen for a guest starring role on one of the most successful television drama series of all time—*ER*.

ER is a medical drama about the day-to-day happenings in a very busy emergency room (or

"ER" for short) set in the fictional County General Hospital located in the Loop area of downtown Chicago. (The area is called the Loop because the tracks of the public transportation elevated trains, or "el trains," that run through the city are on a loop that runs in and out of the downtown business area.)

It was a huge break for Boo Boo. *ER* was a very successful, award-winning television program that had launched the careers of some big-name actors, including heartthrob George Clooney! The show was created by Michael Crichton. Michael Crichton is a best-selling science fiction novelist most famous for penning novels that were later turned into blockbuster movies.

The most famous of all of these is the 1993 Steven Spielberg box office smash *Jurassic Park*, about people who are trapped on an island-turned-amusement-park full of living dinosaurs. The movie, which starred Sam Neill, Laura Dern, Jeff Goldblum, Samuel L. Jackson, and Joseph Mazzello, won Oscars for its groundbreaking CGI special effects, and made more than $914 million dollars at the box office worldwide. In fact, it was the most successful movie ever made at the time, until the movie *Titanic* came along and smashed all existing box-office records in 1997 to become the biggest movie of all time. *Jurassic Park* also spawned two successful sequels, *The Lost World: Jurassic Park* and *Jurassic Park III*.

Another Hollywood movie based on one of Michael Crichton's sci-fi novels is *Sphere*, about the discovery of a spaceship at the bottom of the ocean. The 1998 thriller was directed by Barry Levinson, and starred Dustin Hoffman, Sharon Stone, Queen Latifah, Liev Schreiber, and *Jurassic Park* star Samuel L. Jackson as scientists who go below the sea to investigate a ship (they later find out the ship is actually from the future!). Crichton also wrote original screenplays, such as *Twister*, the 1996 disaster flick about rival storm-chasing scientists who find themselves chasing one of the biggest tornadoes ever. The movie, starring Helen Hunt, Bill Paxton, and Philip Seymour Hoffman, was another big smash at the box office for Crichton.

But in the late 1960s, before he was a famous science fiction writer, Michael Crichton was a student at one of the most renowned medical schools in the country, Harvard Medical School in Boston, Massachusetts. It was there that Crichton became fascinated by medicine and the way it affected people's lives. Eventually, he decided that he was more interested in writing than he was in becoming a doctor, but that didn't mean that he had left the world of medicine completely behind.

Many years later, his experience at Harvard inspired him to write a script for a new television show, *ER*, which not only told stories about the patients who came into the emergency room for treatment, but also about the day-to-day lives of the doctors and nurses who worked at the hospital in such stressful but ultimately rewarding jobs. The show was a huge success, and ran for fifteen seasons on NBC from 1994 to 2009, becoming the longest-running medical series in primetime TV history in the United States. Many famous actors starred in the show, including George Clooney, who went on to star in such box office hits as *Batman and Robin* and *Ocean's Eleven* and both of its sequels, and even won an Academy Award for his role in the thriller

Syriana. And *ER* was also very well respected in the television arts community, winning twenty-three Emmy Awards over the course of the show. In fact, the show went on to earn an amazing total of 123 Emmy nominations—more than any other television show ever!

Boo Boo appeared on the twelfth season of *ER*, in the 2005 episode entitled "Man with No Name." The main story line of that episode involved the head of the ER, Dr. Luka Kova , played by Goran Visnjic, and the terrible day he was having at work. But in a secondary story line, the character of Dr. Archie Morris, played by actor Scott Grimes, who was the chief resident of the ER, was being tormented by a little boy wearing a red Power Ranger costume—and that little boy was none other than Boo Boo! Boo Boo didn't get to use all of his martial arts skills in the role, but it was pretty cool that he got to be a Power Ranger, nonetheless! And he followed in the footsteps of many other actors who had bit parts on the show and went on to greater fame, including Zac Efron (the *High School Musical* movies and *Hairspray*), Vincent Kartheiser (the acclaimed TV drama *Mad Men*), Emile Hirsch (*Speed Racer* and *Into the Wild*), Shia LaBeouf (*Even Stevens, Transformers,* and *Indiana Jones and the Kingdom of the Crystal Skull*)—and even Boo Boo's future *Eclipse* costar, Dakota Fanning!

Boo Boo scored guest roles on other television series, too. His work on *ER* allowed him to find work on other television shows, since the casting directors of those shows knew he had experience. That same year, he landed the recurring role of Stephen on five episodes of *Dante's Cove*, a mature supernatural soap opera, which ran on the cable network Here! from 2004 to 2007. Boo Boo's little sister Fivel also appeared on that show in the same episodes as Boo Boo, in the role of Betty. The next year, in 2006, Boo Boo guest starred in two episodes of the popular sitcom *Everybody Hates Chris*, which started its run on the now-defunct UPN Network in 2005, and then ran on the CW for three more years, before going off the air in 2009.

Everybody Hates Chris was based on the life of hilarious stand-up comedian and actor Chris Rock, and his formative experiences growing up in the somewhat rough Bedford-Stuyvesant area of Brooklyn, New York, also known as Bed-Stuy, in the 1980s. Chris Rock not only came up with the idea for the show and produced it, but he also provided voiceovers for every episode as the narrator. The very talented and funny actor Tyler James Williams starred as a young Chris, and other regular cast members included Terry Crews as Chris's stern, hard-working father, Julius; Tichina Arnold as Chris's tough but loving mother, Rochelle; Tequan Richmond as Chris's popular younger brother, Drew; and Imani Hakim as Chris's sassy younger sister, Tanya.

In the show, Chris is forced to take buses across town to get to his school, Corleone Junior High, which is located in the strongly Italian neighborhood of South Shore—a world away from where Chris and his family live. Much of the humor stems from zany situations that Chris gets into, both at home and at school. He is often blamed for things that aren't really his fault, or are beyond his control, which is why he thinks that everyone hates him!

Since many of the plot lines of the episodes took place at Chris's junior high school, there were a lot of opportunities for talented young actors to appear on the show. Boo Boo appeared in two episodes of *Everybody Hates Chris*. The first episode, "Everybody Hates Playboy," aired in the first season; the second episode, "Everybody Hates Elections," was part of the second season of the show. It must have been so much fun to work on such a funny show, and was probably a great experience for the young actor.

In 2006, Boo Boo got the chance to play a part he was born to play—himself! Boo Boo and his sister Fivel were chosen to host several episodes of *Blue Dolphin Kids*, a syndicated documentary-style show for kids about the tropical islands of Hawaii. The show had a live-action magazine format similar to *Entertainment Tonight* or *Access Hollywood*, with educational trivia and facts mixed together with exciting footage of the natural beauty of Hawaii, the fiftieth state of the United States.

2006 was another busy year for the up-and-coming star. Boo Boo appeared in another film that was screened in festivals, this one called *The Conrad Boys*, about nineteen-year-old Charlie Conrad, who is forced to take care of his nine-year-old brother Ben after their mother passes away. Justin Lo not only played the main character of Charlie, but he also wrote and directed the movie! Boo Boo played little brother Ben, and Nils Sr. was the stunt coordinator for the movie.

That same year, Boo Boo also appeared in *18 Fingers of Death!*, a goofy *Spinal Tap*–esque mockumentary about Buford Lee, a low-budget martial arts star, and the fan who wants to make a documentary about Buford so that his talents will finally be recognized. The straight-to-video movie starred James Lew (who also wrote and directed it) as Buford, and featured appearances by *The Karate Kid*'s Pat Morita and action star Lorenzo Lamas, as well as Nils Sr. in the role of Deadly Thug #1 / Al. Boo Boo got the chance to show off some of his own martial arts moves in the movie, when he appeared as a young version of Buford.

But the biggest break that Boo Boo got in 2006 came in the form of one of his first starring roles! He played the main character in a direct-to-video movie called *666: The Child*. In this eerie-but-funny supernatural thriller, Boo Boo played the role of

Donald, a child who appears to have been the only survivor of a tragic plane crash, and is adopted by new parents who take him in, only to find out he is the son of Satan! Once again, Boo Boo got to work with his father and big sis, Maegan, which must have been nice. Nils Sr. and Maegan both worked as stunt people and provided mechanical effects work for the movie, and Maegan also appeared on-screen as a dental assistant who meets a grisly end.

The movie wasn't well-reviewed by critics, but that's partly because there was a theatrical version of a similar movie out at the same time, the remake of the scary supernatural classic *The Omen*, starring Liev Schreiber and Julia Stiles. But *666: The Child* gave Boo Boo the chance to play a bigger role in a movie, something that he had been dying to do for years. He appreciated all the film and television work that he had done over the past few years, but what he really wanted was to be a star. Even if *666: The Child* wasn't well-received critically, it was still a huge victory for Boo Boo because he was able to play a starring role! Little did he know that soon he would have the chance to work on his very first

Hollywood blockbuster. Talk about a dream come true!

CHAPTER 4

BOO BOO HITS THE BIG SCREEN!

Boo Boo's fledgling acting career was just starting to take off. He continued to land roles in low-budget action movies, including *The Last Sentinel* (2007), about an electronically-enhanced soldier, played by kickboxer Don "The Dragon" Wilson, who helps a resistance fighter played by *Battlestar Galactica*'s Katee Sackhoff. In this movie, Boo Boo once again played a young version of the main character. And then he did it *again* in the 2008 movie *The Fifth Commandment*, this time as a young version of Rick Yune's character, Chance Templeton, an elite assassin who must defend his own life. Obviously, these action stars knew that Boo Boo had what it took to represent them and their characters!

In 2007, there was also the DVD release of *Uncle P*, a comedy starring hip-hop star Master P as a rapper millionaire (just like in real life!) who becomes the guardian of his sister's three kids. The movie also starred Lil' Romeo and Cheech Marin, and Boo Boo appeared as Biker Kid. But Boo Boo was ready for bigger roles, and couldn't wait for the opportunity to show off what he could do. He knew he just needed a big break.

Boo Boo once told *Popstar!* magazine his biggest goal for his movie career: "I want to be an action star." So when he got the opportunity to work on *Beowulf*, the highly anticipated CGI motion capture adaptation of the classic Old English poem of the same name to be directed by Robert Zemeckis, Boo Boo must have jumped at the chance!

Beowulf is the classic story of a warrior hero who arrives in a kingdom just in time to answer the king's call for a hero to fight the demon Grendel, who has attacked and killed many local townspeople. Beowulf battles Grendel and mortally wounds him, but Beowulf must then confront the demon's mother. He eventually becomes king, but then must deal with the tragic events of his past. *Beowulf* is universally considered one of the first, and most important, stories in the history of literature! In fact, many high school students are assigned this story in their literature classes, since it is one of the first known examples of an epic poem (*The Odyssey* is another). So to make the first faithful film version of a classic story that had been around for hundreds of years, the producers decided to pull out all the stops.

The screenplay for the film was written by the brilliant and inventive Neil Gaiman, an author and comic book writer whose books *Stardust*, about a star that falls to Earth, and *Coraline*, about an adventurous little girl who finds a passageway to a secret world, were both turned into big-budget Hollywood movies; *Coraline* (2009) was turned into a 3-D computer animated film, while *Stardust* (2007) featured such Hollywood heavyweights as Michelle Pfeiffer, Robert De Niro, and Claire Danes as the fallen star Yvaine.

"Beowulf is a remarkable, powerful story," Gaiman told moviesonline.ca. "It's the oldest story in the English language that we have. But, it's always been considered incredibly problematic, from a literary and critical point of view, in that it starts with young Beowulf coming in and rescuing [the kingdom] from Grendel and from Grendel's mother, and then we cut fifty years later, and he fights the dragon and dies. That's the poem. What we were trying to do was keep the events of the poem while giving the events a reason to have happened."

The film's renowned director, Robert Zemeckis, has brought more than a dozen movies to the big screen, including over-the-top special-effects blockbusters like the *Back to the Future* trilogy starring Michael J. Fox and the live action/animated film *Who Framed Roger Rabbit* (starring Bob Hoskins along with a huge supporting cast of Warner Brothers and Walt Disney characters, including Mickey Mouse, Donald Duck, Bugs Bunny, and Daffy Duck). These special-effects blockbusters are considered modern classics to today's moviegoers. More recently, Zemeckis had directed a movie version of *The Polar Express*, based on the popular Christmas storybook classic by Chris Van Allsburg.

What was exciting about the movie version of *The Polar Express* was that the director filmed the actors, including superstar Tom Hanks, using computers for a revolutionary hi-tech process that captured all of their motions and movements digitally. This way, the movements of the actors could be used to animate 3-D characters on-screen by the computers. It was like nothing audiences had ever seen before! Robert felt that this new technique was the future of moviemaking, and so he decided he wanted to try it again when he made *Beowulf.*

The director and producers wanted to secure an all-star cast to help them make their version of *Beowulf* into a guaranteed box office hit. So they hired a list of award-winning actors to play many of the major roles in the movie. Anthony Hopkins, best known for his role as the cannibal Dr. Hannibal Lecter in the 1991 thriller *The Silence of the Lambs*, as well as in both its sequel *Hannibal* (2001) and prequel *Red Dragon* (2002), played King Hrothgar; John Malkovich (*Dangerous Liaisons, Con Air*, and *Eragon*) played the warrior Unferth; Crispin Glover (*Back to the Future, Charlie's Angels*, and *Tim Burton's Alice in Wonderland*) played the monster Grendel; and the stunning actress Angelina Jolie was cast as the monster's mother.

Actor Ray Winstone (who voiced the role of Mr. Beaver in *The Chronicles of Narnia: The Lion, the Witch and the Wardrobe*) was cast to play Beowulf as an adult, but they also needed someone to play Beowulf as a young boy. Luckily, the fight choreographer for the movie was Dominiquie Vandenberg—who had already appeared in both *Skeleton Man* and *Pit Fighter* with Boo Boo. He must have known that Boo Boo would be absolutely perfect for the part, and so Boo Boo was able to step right up and nab the role!

Boo Boo must have been totally excited to finally land a part in such a big Hollywood movie—especially one where he got to show off his martial arts training! "I really like doing stunts and wire work," he told *Teen Scene* magazine about his stunt work as the young hero on *Beowulf.* "It was fun." Kidzworld.com also asked Boo Boo about his experiences on the movie, and he told them: "We did wire works. I had to do a scene where I had to run up this guy and spin. It was really fun, it was a little crazy!" Sounds like a whole lot of fun, especially for a gifted athlete like Boo Boo!

Boo Boo must have been super-excited when he found out that Angelina Jolie was going to be in *Beowulf,* since she is one of his favorite actresses! Unfortunately, Boo Boo never actually got the chance to meet her while working on the movie, since the character of Beowulf doesn't encounter Grendel's mother until he's an adult. "No, Angelina Jolie filmed everything separately, so I never got to meet her," Boo Boo told kidzworld.com. "I did meet Crispin Glover though!"

The filming process was a new experience for all of the actors, but since they were only providing the essence of the performances, and the actual characters who appear on-screen would later be created by computers, it seemed to give the actors the freedom to try new things and get carried away with the story! Ray Winstone told moviesonline.ca that he loved it: "You were allowed to go, like theater, where you carry a scene on and you become engrossed within the scene . . . You actually cracked on with a scene and your energy levels were kept up . . . I would love to do this again sometime because I think it's going to get better, and better, and better."

Crispin Glover had another challenge with his performance: His character, Grendel, speaks only in Old English—which is very different than the English we speak today! "We had a professor that we got to sit down with, who helped figure out what was actually said in Old English," Crispin told moviesonline.ca. "It was written in modern English, and then it made sense for Grendel to be the one that speaks in complete Old English." So for Crispin, it was like learning a completely new—or old—language!

Luckily, all of the actors' and crew members' hard work and dedication paid off. The movie got a ton of rave reviews for its amazing 3-D animation and was a number one smash at the box office, bringing in almost $200 million worldwide. And it gave Boo Boo his first taste of box office success with a big fantasy-action blockbuster . . . but that was only a hint of what was to come for him in the future!

CHAPTER 5

Not only is Boo Boo a talented actor and martial artist, but he can also sing and dance and even play guitar—making him a quintuple threat in the entertainment business! In fact, Boo Boo is an accomplished musical performer, having performed as a backup singer and dancer for one of the hottest superstars around, Miley Cyrus!

Boo Boo's first taste of musical success was with the T-Squad, a supergroup of performers who were signed to Walt Disney Records. Disney has a long history of making teen singers into superstars, starting way back in the 1950s! That was when the original *The Mickey Mouse Club* television show first aired, creating stars out of young Mouseketeers like Annette Funicello.

After audiences got to know her as a Mouseketeer, Annette released several hit records throughout the '50s and '60s, and then went on to star in a series of "beach party" movies, which cemented her status as one of the original teen idols. Annette later went on to do commercials for Skippy peanut butter, and has become a spokesperson and active fund-raiser for many important causes like medical research, including the disease multiple sclerosis, or MS, which she has lived with for many years. Annette is still a beloved icon of the entertainment industry over fifty years after she got her start—which just goes to show that Walt Disney knew what he was doing when he gave her that first big break!

The television show *The Mickey Mouse Club* went through several reinventions over the years, most notably with *The All New Mickey Mouse Club*, which began in 1989 and ran until its cancellation in 1994. *The All New Mickey Mouse Club*, or *MMC*, as it was known, was revived by the Disney Channel with a new format inspired by the success of other popular shows for kids, such as the hit *You Can't Do That on Television*, which ran on cable channel Nickelodeon from 1979 to 1990. Since the show now featured a mixture of live skits, prerecorded comedy segments, and musical performances, they needed to find versatile performers who could sing, act, and dance—in other words, they needed a performer just like Boo Boo!

MMC proved to be an amazing predictor of young talented artists, which included both actors and musicians. One of the earliest signs that *MMC*'s performers were more than just television stars was when five of the cast members branched out to form a musical group called the Party in 1992. Together, Damon Pampolina, Tiffini Hale, Chase Hampton, Albert Fields, and Deedee Magno went on to release a total of four albums together, and they had a radio hit with the song "In My Dreams." But that was only the beginning of the success the roster of *MMC* would see!

The show featured many different cast members over the course of its run, including a handful of young actors who would go on to success as adults, like Keri Russell and Ryan Gosling. After guest appearances on shows like *Boy Meets World* and *7th Heaven,* Keri became famous for her role as the delightful college student Felicity Porter on the WB drama *Felicity,* which ran from 1998 to 2002. Keri won a Golden Globe Award for her work on the show, and has gone on to act in a variety of movies including the blockbuster *Mission: Impossible III* (2006) with Tom Cruise, the 2007 independent film *Waitress*, the touching drama *August Rush* (also 2007) with Robin Williams and Freddie Highmore, and the hilarious 2008 comedy *Bedtime Stories* with Adam Sandler. She even provided the voice of one of the most famous superheroes of all time, Wonder Woman, in an animated movie that came out on DVD in 2009!

Ryan Gosling is considered among the most talented actors of his generation. He has appeared in movies such as the 2000 historical football drama *Remember the Titans* with Denzel Washington and the chilling 2002 thriller *Murder by Numbers* with Sandra Bullock, and is probably best known for his romantic leading turn as Noah in the smash 2004 hit *The Notebook*, which also starred Rachel McAdams. Ryan went on to win a Spirit Award for his role as a struggling junior high school teacher in the 2006 drama *Half Nelson*, and he was even nominated for an Academy Award for the film! And not only is he keeping busy with his career as an award-winning actor, but Ryan is also keeping his musical muscles flexed, as well! His band, Dead Man's Bones, recorded and released a self-titled album, which they recorded with the Silverlake Conservatory of Music's children's choir.

But Ryan isn't the only *MMC* graduate to keep making music as an adult. In fact, *MMC* might be responsible for some of the biggest superstars in the world of music today! Mouseketeers from the show who went on to find mega-success on the charts include none other than Justin Timberlake, Britney Spears, and Christina Aguilera—singers who began as teen idols and have become Grammy Award–winning superstars and perpetual Billboard chart toppers!

Justin Timberlake first found fame as part of the boy band 'N Sync. Justin, along with fellow members JC Chasez, Lance Bass, Joey Fatone, and Chris Kirkpatrick, formed the group in Orlando, Florida, in 1995. They went on to release multiple top ten albums, including the 2000 release *No Strings Attached*, which sold a record 2.4 million copies in its first week, and over 9.9 million copies by the end of that year. After the group decided to take some time off, Justin went on to release two hit solo albums, *Justified* and *FutureSex/LoveSounds*, and chart-topping singles including "Cry Me a River," "SexyBack," and "My Love." Justin has also collaborated with many of pop music's biggest names, including the Black Eyed Peas, Snoop Dogg, Timbaland, Ciara, and Madonna.

Justin's ex-girlfriend Britney has done pretty well for herself, too. Her debut single ". . . Baby One More Time," debuted at number 1 on the pop charts in 1999, as did the album of the same name. And her next three albums, *Oops! . . . I Did It Again* (2000), *Britney* (2001), and *In the Zone* (2003) all followed suit, setting a record for consecutive debuts at the top of the charts. Her videos for songs like "Toxic," "Piece of Me," and "Womanizer" have kept her in heavy rotation on MTV, and she has also branched out into the world of fragrances, with several Elizabeth Arden perfumes becoming big sellers.

Christina Aguilera also released her self-titled debut album in 1999, followed by *Stripped* (2002) and *Back to Basics* (2006). Her hit singles include "Genie in a Bottle," "What a Girl Wants," "Beautiful," and "Ain't No Other Man," as well as her all-star collaboration with recording artists Mya, Pink, and Lil' Kim for the cover of Patty LaBelle's classic "Lady Marmalade," which was recorded for the soundtrack to the movie musical *Moulin Rouge!* (starring Nicole Kidman and Ewan McGregor) in 2001. Christina is also known for her colorful, fun music videos, including such clips as "Come on Over Baby (All I Want Is You)," "Dirrty," "Candyman," and "Keeps Gettin' Better." She is also a multiple Grammy Award–winner, including having taken home the trophy for Best New Artist back in 2000.

As amazing as the musical legacy of *The All New Mickey Mouse Club* has been, those aren't the only success stories of young musicians who got their big breaks working for Walt Disney. Hilary Duff began her successful career on the Disney Channel as the lead character in the hit sitcom *Lizzie McGuire*, before going on to release songs on the soundtrack to both the TV show and later *The Lizzie McGuire*

Movie. She then went on to release several hit albums—her first one, *Metamorphosis*, hit number 1 on the charts! Some of her many hit singles include "So Yesterday," "Come Clean," and "With Love." Hilary also continues to juggle her music career with acting, recently appearing as the super-famous actress Olivia Burke on the CW TV series *Gossip Girl.* (That role must not have been much of a stretch for her to imagine!)

Another one of the biggest hit makers on the music charts these days is Miley Cyrus, who became almost instantly famous for her starring role on *Hannah Montana* on the Disney Channel. The series, about an average preteen schoolgirl named Miley Stewart who lives a secret double life as a famous pop singer named Hannah Montana, began in 2006 and inspired a concert tour and a smash theatrical release in 2009 called *Hannah Montana: The Movie.* And much like her character on the TV show, Miley has had a double career on the pop charts—with hits as both Hannah ("Best of Both Worlds") and as herself, with her songs "The Climb" and "Party in the U.S.A." becoming top ten hits!

And of course, no discussion of Walt Disney's chart toppers would be complete without mentioning the *High School Musical* albums! Each of the soundtracks for the three movies, starring Zac Efron, Vanessa Hudgens, Ashley Tisdale, Corbin Bleu, Lucas Grabeel, and Monique Coleman, has topped the charts and been certified gold, a high honor in the music industry, which means that an album has shipped more than 500,000 copies! The soundtracks also set records—when the first soundtrack came out, nine of the songs hit the Billboard Hot 100 chart at once. The Billboard Hot 100 measures the most popular songs in the country each week. Never before had nine songs from the same album all been on the chart at once! That's quite an accomplishment!

So when Boo Boo found himself performing on the Disney Channel, he had to have known he was in good company. But first, Boo Boo had to become good enough at singing and dancing to make the cut—not every budding singer and actor has the kind of "star quality" that Disney is looking for! Boo Boo started dancing when he was around ten years old, and has showcased his dancing talents in the video for rap superstar Eminem's hit "Just Lose It," as well as backup dancing for the singing duo the EriAm Sisters for their quarterfinal appearance on the NBC hit series *America's Got Talent*, and dancing as part of the cast of the *Camp Rock Freestyle Jam* on Disney. And Boo Boo has known for a long time that he wanted to be a singer. But most performers aren't as lucky (or as driven) as Boo Boo—he was signed to his record deal with Walt Disney Records when he was only twelve years old!

CHAPTER 6

T-SQUAD POWERS, ACTIVATE!

So how did Boo Boo join the T-Squad and land a major record deal at only twelve years old? Boo Boo told *Teen Scene* magazine: "I was asked to audition for a group." The audition he spoke of was for a woman named Colleen Fitzpatrick, a producer who was in the process of looking for recording artists to work with. Colleen was no stranger to the music business—in fact, she's recorded hit records herself! After acting in movies like John Waters's original *Hairspray* (which later inspired the remade musical of the same name starring John Travolta and Zac Efron), Colleen started her career in the music industry in an alternative rock band named Eve's Plum (after the actress Eve Plumb, who starred as middle sister Jan Brady on the classic sitcom *The Brady Bunch*). When Eve's Plum broke up, Colleen decided to try her hand at pop music. She decided to call herself Vitamin C, and recorded a solo album.

Before releasing her own album, Vitamin C recorded songs for soundtracks of movies like *Pokemon: The First Movie*, and then released her first single, which was called "Smile." The song eventually hit number 18 on the pop charts. But it was her second single that *really* made Vitamin C famous. "Graduation (Friends Forever)" was also a top 40 hit when it was initially released in 2000, but then the following year in 2001, the song started to get a lot of airplay during the months of May and June. This was no coincidence: May and June are the months when most junior high and high school graduations take place. In fact, for years after its release, the song became somewhat of a tradition for graduates, and was a very popular choice at both graduation parties and commencement ceremonies. The song was even featured in movies (*Scary Movie 2*) and TV shows (*Daria*).

So years later, when Colleen set out to assemble a new band of young, rising superstars, she had an ace up her sleeve: She knew from the outset that she wanted the new group to record its own version of "Graduation (Friends Forever)." After all, the song had proven to be incredibly popular with listeners for years after its release. Why not see if lightning would strike twice?

Colleen must have auditioned many talented kids in her search for a new group. But in the end, she chose four very talented performers that she had to know would be an amazing combination together. The group, which was christened the Truth Squad but later shortened to T-Squad, consisted of actress Miki Ishikawa, dancer Jade Gilley, rapper Taylor McKinney, and, of course, the youngest of the group, an aspiring actor and martial artist known as Boo Boo Stewart!

This new group had a special purpose in addition to entertaining, as they explained on their MySpace page: "The T-Squad is a vocal and dance hip-hop /pop-'super group'-comprised of four uniquely talented young performers that individually have mad skills in dance, electrifying vocals, and an unbelievable presence. They also share a unifying desire to show the people the TRUTH and expose dishonesty. Pledging to stick together through thick and thin, the Truth Squad has set out to show how friendship and trust are the keys to a better world and best of all, they do it all through phat beats and tight moves. Each Truth Squad member has spent years working, honing their craft and starring in feature films, TV shows, commercials, print ads, singing on albums, and performing before millions. But 'super star' résumés are not enough; these four kids understand the value of positive thinking, diversity, and hard work. All of them have exciting individual careers but recognize the value of working as a group to spread the truth!"

Like Boo Boo, Miki Ishikawa began performing at a very early age—six years old! She had already appeared in a recurring role as Vicky on the hit Nickelodeon TV show *Zoey 101*. Her first feature film role was as Naoko North in the romantic comedy *Yours, Mine and Ours*, which also starred Dennis Quaid and Rene Russo.

Jade Gilley is a very accomplished young dancer who has competed in national dance competitions, helping her group win multiple national titles. Jade appeared as a backup dancer in music videos for superstars like rapper Missy Elliot and Gwen

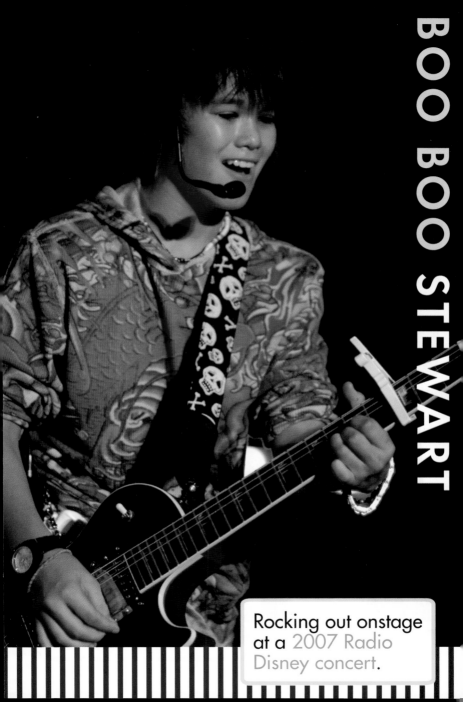

BOO BOO STEWART

Rocking out onstage at a 2007 Radio Disney concert.

red carpet pose at the 2008 premiere of *Kung Fu Panda*.

BOO BOO takes time out for his adoring fans.

Taking time off to volunteer for a good cause.

BOO BOO hangs with his band, Echoes of Angels, at his fourteenth birthday party!

Looking cute on the red carpet with sis **FIVEL** at the premiere of *Twilight Saga: New Moon*.

Stefani, and live onstage alongside the popular hip-hop group Outkast at the 2004 Nickelodeon Kids' Choice Awards. And in addition to her dancing, Jade also managed to earn straight As as a student! Sounds a lot like Boo Boo!

Taylor McKinney, who also goes by the performing name Kid Karizz, has appeared on the gritty FX police drama *The Shield,* and in a televised Christmas special with Oscar-winning actor and talented musician and comedian Jamie Foxx. With his indispensable rapping skills, Karizz was the perfect fourth member of the T-Squad!

To help them develop and get to know one another as a group, T-Squad went on tour to open for the Disney group the Cheetah Girls. One of the other opening acts? Rising superstar Hannah Montana! T-Squad was also asked to be a part of the Radio Disney Jingle Jam tour with Hannah Montana and the Jonas Brothers in 2006! "It was really sad when it was over," Boo Boo told *Teen* magazine. "There's hardly ever a serious moment when we're together. We still get the work done, but there are laughs every now and then."

Speaking of getting the work done, T-Squad still had an album to record! Going on tour took up a lot of their time, but they made sure to get back in the studio as soon as possible. They spent a lot of time in the recording studio, and on December 12, 2006, their first single "Vertical" was released. The song appeared on the soundtrack to the Disney original TV movie *Jump In!*, the story of a young boxer who discovers his love of the jump rope style double Dutch. *Jump In!* starred Corbin Bleu from *High School Musical* and recording artist Keke Palmer, the star of Nickelodeon's hit television show *True Jackson, VP*. Both Keke and Corbin also appeared on the movie's soundtrack. T-Squad must have been pretty excited to have been included in their company!

Soon after their appearance on the *Jump In!* soundtrack, the group's self-titled album *T-Squad* was released on April 3, 2007. In addition to the inclusion of "Vertical" from *Jump In!*, the album featured several other songs that would go on to become Radio Disney hit singles, including "Flip," "No Sleep 'Til Summertime," and their cover of "Graduation (Friends Forever)." Other songs on the album included "Roc da Mic," "Believe," "Journey's Just Begun," "Me Likey," "Where the Heart Is," "Trust," and "What'cha Gonna Do?"

"All the songs are so different. Some are slow, fast, upbeat . . . I love the song 'Flip.' It's the best one on the album, I think," Boo Boo said to *Teen* magazine. And if he loved the song, he must have had a blast filming the video, too! Kid Karizz told *Teen* magazine: "We're all flipping around on harnesses. We were jumping from building to building, and it was kind of like we were superheroes, having fun and doing karate moves. It was really fun." Sounds like it must have been right up Boo Boo's alley!

The T-Squad album also included a cover version of "Parents Just Don't Understand," a song originally recorded by the hip-hop duo DJ Jazzy Jeff & the Fresh Prince in the '80s. The Fresh Prince would later become better known by his real name, Will Smith. Will branched out to star in his own comedy on NBC, *The Fresh Prince of Bel-Air*, about a smart, streetwise young boy from Philadelphia who moved to the ritzy neighborhood of Bel-Air in California to live with his well-to-do aunt and uncle. The show ran from 1990 to 1996, and won multiple NAACP Image Awards, and Will himself took home a Blimp Award for Favorite TV Actor at the 1991 Nickelodeon Kids' Choice Awards.

After his sitcom success, Will did continue to make hit records, but he soon became better known as one of the most successful actors at the box office. Throughout the '90s and into the '00s, Will starred in box office hit after box office hit, including the action buddy comedy *Bad Boys* (1995) and its later sequel (in 2003) with Martin Lawrence, the 1998 thriller *Enemy of the State*, and most notably a string of sci-fi special effects bonanzas, including *Independence Day* (1996), *Men in Black* (1997) and *Men in Black II* (2002), *Wild Wild West* (1999), *I, Robot* (2004), and *I Am Legend* (2007). But Will also went on to star in serious dramas, too, earning Academy Award nominations for his roles in the true-life biopics *Ali* (2001), about championship boxer Cassius Clay, who was better known as Muhammad Ali, and *The Pursuit of Happyness* (2006). Will Smith is someone whose career Boo Boo probably wouldn't mind modeling his own after!

One other song that T-Squad included on their album was "Second Star to the Right." This song was notable because it was originally written for the animated Walt Disney classic *Peter Pan*. What a nice way for this latest group of Disney performers to pay their respects to the classic Disney films they probably grew up watching!

Soon after T-Squad dropped their album, the group got to experience the next phase of becoming musicians: going on a tour of their own. T-Squad was the headlining act for the Disneymania Concerts for Conservation, a ten-city tour of zoos and aquariums that helped to raise money for conservation efforts. The 2007 tour, sponsored by the Association of Zoos and Aquariums, was presented by Build-A-Bear. In addition to entertaining ticket payers with singing and dancing, the tour helped to educate attendees about conservation efforts and provided information about animals and their natural habitats. Chris Warren Jr. and Olesya Rulin, who played Zeke and Kelsi in *High School Musical* and its sequels, were asked to be the emcees of the tour.

"I love touring: the travel, the hotels, and the

shows," Boo Boo told *Teen Scene* magazine. Although sometimes the fans can get a little too carried away! "I was at a football game one time and when we were walking away, we had to run like crazy 'cause all these fans had my arm!" Boo Boo told kidzworld.com. "They were trying to rip my arm off and we were running and running." It's a good thing Boo Boo got away from those fans in one piece!

Boo Boo also knows how tricky it can be to focus on performing in front of screaming fans. "Once onstage during a concert, my mic[rophone] got caught in my jacket," Boo Boo told *Popstar!* magazine. "My wallet chain pulled on the mic cord and got wrapped up in my blazer. I struggled to get the jacket off without losing the mic, all while my head was being pulled backward because of the wires." That would have been a sight to see! But it obviously wasn't a deterrent to Boo Boo, who just kept on going.

"I went on tour with Miley Cyrus, Jonas Brothers, Demi Lovato," Boo Boo told *Access Hollywood*. He must have really enjoyed being out on the road, performing to packed audiences every night! Back when he was first getting started, Boo Boo probably never could have imagined that his music career would lead him to such success, performing in front of screaming fans night after night. But it was surely a goal of his, and one that he accomplished at a very early age!

Boo Boo must have gotten along pretty well with Miley and the Jonas Brothers because he's also appeared in commercials with them for Danimals yogurt and Target stores. In fact, Boo Boo has appeared in quite a lot of advertising over the course of his career, for Kohl's and JCPenney department stores, Levi's, Kodak, Guess, H&M, Nintendo Wii, and McDonald's, among other brands.

After the T-Squad finished touring for their record, the group members decided to go their separate ways and pursue their own projects. Boo Boo decided to take advantage of this opportunity, and branch out a bit musically. He recently formed a new rock band called Echoes of Angels, which should be a great outlet for his guitar playing! The band has posted clips of their performances on YouTube, including the original songs "Fridays" and

"We Were Just So Right," as well as rocking covers of songs by bands like REO Speedwagon ("Only the Strong Survive"), Guns N' Roses ("Sweet Child O' Mine"), Alice in Chains ("Man in the Box"), Paul McCartney and Wings ("Live and Let Die"), and Modern English ("I Melt with You" from the 1983 movie *Valley Girl*).

Boo Boo has also been performing with his sisters Maegan and Fivel as TSC (The Stewart Clan), and in 2008, Boo Boo and Fivel recorded a video that showcased their singing and dancing, called "Turn It Up." Boo Boo also recorded the theme song for the Disney Channel Games in 2008, and a solo album with Disney is also a possibility for the future. It seems Boo Boo isn't content with just one type of music—he wants to find many outlets for his musical creativity, which means more opportunities for his fans to listen to him!

CHAPTER 7

THE SEARCH FOR SETH CLEARWATER

Boo Boo had already accomplished quite a bit for a young star, but the best was yet to come. In 2009, Boo Boo encountered his most exciting project to date: He found out that the role of the werewolf Seth Clearwater was about to be cast for *The Twilight Saga: Eclipse*, and he knew that he had to go for it! *Eclipse* was based on the third book in the wildly popular *Twilight* series of supernatural romance books by Stephenie Meyer. The first two films in the series, *Twilight* (2008) and *The Twilight Saga: New Moon* (2009), had already made megastars out of Robert Pattinson, Kristen Stewart (who isn't related to Boo Boo, even though they have the same last name), and Taylor Lautner, Boo Boo's old friend from their XMA training days. Boo Boo had to have known that taking a role in one of the Twilight Saga movies would skyrocket him to superstardom.

When he decided to try out for the role, Boo

Boo also knew that his fans were super-excited about the idea of him playing the character of Seth, one of the youngest members of the La Push pack of werewolves. In fact, he probably even had some of them to thank for helping him in his quest for the role! Before the newest roles for *The Twilight Saga: Eclipse* were even cast, some of Boo Boo's most vocal fans started posting videos on YouTube, explaining why he would be perfect for the part of Seth.

Seth Clearwater, like his older sister Leah Clearwater, is a member of the La Push pack of werewolves, who are actually shape-shifters. Seth idolizes Jacob Black, and is said to remind Bella of a younger Jacob—just like some fans have said that Boo Boo reminds them of a younger Taylor Lautner! Seth is also the only werewolf who initially feels comfortable being around the Cullen family of vampires, and Edward, who can read minds, says that Seth has very honest and pure thoughts. But while he gets along with Edward and his family, Seth is also very loyal to Jacob.

One YouTube poster named Caitlin was among the first of Boo Boo's fans to post a video online in support of her favorite star for the role of Seth. On May 31, 2009, Caitlin posted a video with a montage of dozens of photos of Boo Boo in his coolest martial arts poses, and said, "I think Boo Boo Stewart should play Seth in the Twilight Movies. He's 15 like Seth. He's really good looking. He does martial arts like Taylor used too. They know each other because they both trained at/with XMA. I think Boo Boo would be perfect. What do you think?"

Caitlin even posted a link in the comments section to a website with information about the casting process for *Eclipse,* in hopes that Boo Boo would read it and decide to audition! She was determined to convince Boo Boo that he should be the one to play Seth—and it worked! *Popstar!* magazine posted on Twitter that "Boo Boo says it was a fan who told him he should try out for the role of Seth Clearwater that first got him interested." Boo Boo was on MySpace one day, and a fan contacted him and told him about the video, and the casting opportunity for the part of Seth Clearwater.

Boo Boo was obviously aware of what a big hit the first *Twilight* movie had been—after all, it was a huge smash at the box office, making over $380 million worldwide! The movie, released in 2007, was directed by Catherine Hardwicke, and starred Kristen Stewart as Bella Swan, the down-to-earth high school student who finds herself caught in an unexpected—and dangerous—romance with the mysterious vampire Edward Cullen. And Taylor Lautner, whom Boo Boo had known since he was ten years old, starred as Jacob Black, the sweet Native American boy who also has feelings for Bella. Audiences fell in love with the movie, and its story of how Bella found herself in a growing love triangle with the vampire Edward and the shape-shifting werewolf Jacob.

A huge part of why the movie did so well at the box office was obviously that the talented cast did such a great job bringing these fantastic characters to life on the big screen. And it's not surprising, considering the experience that these actors had before landing their roles! Kristen Stewart had starred in the 2002 thriller *Panic Room* with Jodie Foster, and also appeared in the wild adventure movie *Zathura: A Space Adventure* (2005) and the true-life story *Into the Wild* (2007), directed by Sean Penn. Robert Pattinson was probably best known for his pivotal role as the heroic Cedric Diggory in two of the blockbuster films in the Harry Potter series, *Harry Potter and the Goblet of Fire* (2005) and *Harry Potter and the Order of the Phoenix* (2007), based on the widly popular book series by J. K. Rowling. And Taylor Lautner was familiar to young audiences from his breakout starring role in the Robert Rodriguez–directed 2005 special effects hit *The Adventures of Sharkboy and Lavagirl 3-D*.

In fact, the *Twilight* books and now the fledgling movie franchise were both becoming so successful that fans were clamoring for all kinds of keepsakes and souvenirs. Toy company Mattel, who manufactures the classic Barbie line of fashion dolls, even created a special pair of Bella and Edward *Twilight* Barbie dolls, modeled after Kristen and Robert!

As Boo Boo learned more about the *Twilight* franchise, and how successful it had become, he likely learned that all four of the books in the series by Stephenie Meyer had spent months and months on the *New York Times* Best Sellers list—a huge feat for any author, as that list is considered the standard for what makes a "hit" in the publishing industry. *Eclipse* was also ranked number 1 on *Publishers Weekly*'s list of "Bestselling Hardcover Backlist Children's Books" in 2008, with over 4.5 million copies sold! That's a lot of fans just waiting to see their favorite story come to life on the silver screen!

So of course, Boo Boo decided to work hard to familiarize himself with the plotline and the character of Seth before he tried out for the role. "For the audition I wanted to be really prepared and know the story, so I read the books," Boo Boo told about.com. And he loved them! "Stephenie Meyer— she did a great job, you know? They can't be any better. They're amazing." Fans worldwide would agree, Boo Boo!

According to Summit Entertainment, the company that produces and distributes the *Twilight* movies, the plot of the movie version of *The Twilight Saga: Eclipse* involves Bella once again finding herself surrounded by danger as the nearby Seattle area suffers a string of mysterious murders. Not to mention the fact that she has to worry about a dangerous vampire who is out for revenge. Bella has to choose between her love for her gorgeous vampire boyfriend Edward and her friendship with superbuff, supersweet werewolf Jacob—knowing that her decision could bring the eternal struggle between vampire and werewolf to a head.

Boo Boo knew that he wanted the part of Seth from the get-go. Not only would it be cool to be a part of the La Push tribe of werewolves, which would probably allow him to show off some of his martial arts skills in the movie, but it was also great that the character of Seth had no problem with the vampires—he's a really nice guy, just like Boo Boo! "Seth is the type of guy who can just walk into the room and make you happy and smile," he told *Popstar!* magazine. "He seems like an all-around good guy; he's a peacemaker." What a great role to play—no wonder Boo Boo decided that he wanted to try and land that part in particular.

When actors try out for a part, it can be a long process. Sometimes they'll have to meet with a casting director, and then read lines from the script. Often, they'll have to come back again to meet with additional people involved with the movie to get their approval, too. These additional meetings are called "callbacks." Eventually, for those actors who are talented and lucky enough, they'll get to meet with the main people in charge of the movie—the director, the producers, and sometimes even the heads of the movie studio! But Boo Boo actually got his foot in the door through a brand-new casting process, which utilizes Internet technology to streamline the process for the executives involved.

Perhaps inspired by the popularity of YouTube, where aspiring actors and actresses often post highlight reels of their work, Cast It Systems is an online casting tool where studios and networks can post information on the roles they're trying to cast. Then, actors can upload videos and their résumés, so that the people making the decision can review them online. It can be a much faster process for the studios, since the casting people don't need to meet with every single actor in person. And it is also helpful for actors who might be on a movie or television set somewhere across the country, or even around the world!

Cast It Systems held exclusive online open calls for actors who wanted to try out for parts in *The Twilight Saga: Eclipse*, so Boo Boo submitted a video of himself and uploaded his résumé to the website for the part of Seth. Turns out, his submission was exactly what the *Eclipse* team was looking for! "I really hit it off with the casting directors," Boo Boo told *Popstar!* magazine. "We did the lines twice and talked the rest of the time. People ask me if I had to act like a wolf in the audition, which I didn't." It seems the producers must have been waiting for someone as talented and perfect for the role as Boo Boo was, because his was the very last audition for the role of Seth that they saw! "I was the last one to audition for the part," Boo Boo told *J-14* magazine, "and when I got the call [my family and I] were all screaming and jumping." How exciting that must have been for Boo Boo and his family! As he told *Lunchbox* magazine, "I can't even put into words how honored I am to be a part of this phenomenon."

Boo Boo wasn't the only new cast member to join the *Twilight* series for *Eclipse*, either. Another key role cast through Cast It's online open call was that of Seth's older sister and fellow werewolf, Leah Clearwater, to be played by Julia Jones. Julia has modeled for such brands as the Gap, L'Oréal, Esprit, and Levi's, and appeared in four 2008 episodes of the TV show *ER* as Dr. Kaya Montoya.

Also new to the cast of the Twilight Saga was Jodelle Ferland as Bree, a young vampire who factors into the future of the story. Jodelle has appeared in many TV shows and movies, most notably the 2004 Stephen King horror series *Kingdom Hospital* on ABC, and the dual role of Sharon/Alessa in the 2006 horror adaptation of the creepy video game *Silent Hill.*

Boo Boo was told he'd have to be on the set in Vancouver, British Columbia, to start filming in mid-September of 2009. At only fifteen years old, he knew he was one of the youngest actors on the set, but he had to be happy to know that his old friend and XMA buddy Taylor Lautner would be there to welcome him. Boo Boo told *Access Hollywood* that he also knew Taylor from singing and dancing classes that they had taken together years before, when both of them were just getting their starts in the business. "He's a really cool guy, and he's really fun to work with," Boo Boo told *Popstar!* magazine about Taylor. But in the meantime, Boo Boo had other things to think about—like preparing to play the part of Seth!

For one thing, Boo Boo wasn't sure how he would need to look for the movie, so he started to consider his hairstyle and his appearance—how would David Slade, who had been signed on to direct the movie, want Seth to look? After all, David had directed lots of cool music videos, as well as 2007's stylish vampire thriller *30 Days of Night*, based on the graphic novel of the same name, about a town in Alaska that gets cut off from the rest of the world when darkness falls for a month in the heart of winter. The main character in *30 Days of Night* was Sheriff Eben Oleson, played by Josh Hartnett, also the star of 2001's World War II action blockbuster *Pearl Harbor* and 2005's *Sin City*, another hit movie based on a graphic novel. Boo Boo must have guessed that someone with David's directing background would have a very specific image in mind for what he wanted everything to look like, down to the last detail.

So what did Boo Boo do? He decided not to get any more haircuts, for one thing! "To prep for *Twilight*, I'm not cutting my hair, I'm just letting it grow out," Boo Boo told the tween gossip website justjaredjr.com. He also explained that he had begun a strict workout regimen to prepare for his role in the film, which involved going to the gym almost every day. "My mom is a personal trainer so she's working me out." How handy to have a trainer for a mom, when you're preparing to play a buff werewolf in a sure-to-be blockbuster movie!

So how did Boo Boo prepare to get his body in shape to look super-ripped like the rest of the wolf pack in the movie? Boo Boo and his mom, Renee, told thesocialife.blogspot.com that he stuck to a strict healthy diet to help himself get into shape. For breakfast, he would have eggs and toast, followed by a mid-morning snack of Muscle Milk. "I love Muscle Milk!" Boo Boo told the blog. For lunch, he would eat steak, brown rice, and a salad, with some chicken breast for his afternoon snack. (Protein helps to build muscles!) Dinner would likely consist of something along the lines of what Boo Boo had for lunch earlier that day, such as steak with brown rice and a salad. He was very careful not to eat any carbohydrates after 6:00 PM, and he also took a teen multivitamin every day.

As far as his exercise routine at the gym, Boo Boo committed himself to a routine of twenty minutes of cardio activity, like running on the treadmill or the elliptical, for at least three days a week, plus weight training. In order to build up muscle, trainer Renee recommends fewer reps, or repetitions, with heavier weights. But if you're trying to build lean muscle like Boo Boo, more reps with lighter weights is the way to go. Renee also stressed that stretching is a necessity! And when thesocialife.blogspot.com asked about Boo Boo's favorite exercise? "I love handstand push ups!" He also did lots of hanging leg raises to help develop those famous abs of his. It sure looks like all that hard work paid off! Boo Boo was ready to tackle the role of Seth, both mentally and physically. It was time to head to the set!

CHAPTER 8
ECLIPSE RISING

The Twilight Saga: Eclipse began production on August 17, 2009, with a target release date of June 30, 2010. Most of the continuing Twilight Saga cast must have still been in character, since filming on the previous movie, *New Moon*, finished only a couple months before, on May 29, 2009. But Boo Boo was just as anxious to dive into the process and begin working with David Slade, the latest director in the franchise, who was following in the footsteps of previous directors Catherine Hardwicke (for *Twilight*) and Chris Weitz (for *The Twilight Saga: New Moon*). Boo Boo told backstage.com that he really liked working with David Slade: "He was incredible, a hilarious guy. He's really cool, just a really nice person. Everyone on set was extremely nice and I just had a great time."

It seems the rest of the cast really liked working with the director, too. Kirsten Prout, who plays Lucy, one of the vampires that "turned" Jasper, said he was a great director. "He's a great guy because his way of working is so open," Kirsten told iesb.net. "He just says, 'Do what you do,' and lets you play with it. If he has notes (on the performance), he gives them to you, but he's a very open director. He keeps it light. He loves his job and he's very serious about it."

Fortunately for Boo Boo, the cast also got along really well with one another! Ashley Greene, who plays the fashionista vampire Alice Cullen, told *Popstar!* magazine, "It's funny, we work fourteen hours together and then we get off work and still hang out together. I don't know how we haven't gotten mad at each other!" Sounds like Boo Boo got really lucky to have joined such a great cast who all get along so well!

In addition to Boo Boo in his role as Seth, the other members of the cast of *The Twilight Saga: Eclipse* include Kristen Stewart as Bella Swan, Robert Pattinson as Edward Cullen, Taylor Lautner as Jacob Black, Billy Burke as Charlie Swan, Ashley Greene as Alice Cullen, Jackson Rathbone as Jasper Hale, Nikki Reed as Rosalie Hale, Kellan Lutz as Emmett Cullen,

Elizabeth Reaser as Esme Cullen, Peter Facinelli as Dr. Carlisle Cullen, Gil Birmingham as Billy Black, Anna Kendrick as Jessica, Dakota Fanning as Jane, and Bryce Dallas Howard as the newly recast evil vampire Victoria (the role was played by Rachelle Lefevre in the first two movies).

In fact, Bryce sounded very excited about her role, and especially the climactic scene at the end of the movie. "There's quite an extraordinary finale," Bryce told *MTV News*. "That was very fun to do. The producers were saying it's the biggest spectacle filmed this far in this franchise. There's a newborn army that's been raised for battle. It's a true battle scene." Jackson Rathbone also spilled the beans to *MTV News* that in *Eclipse*, "We get to go back into Jasper's backstory." Jackson said that he got to shoot scenes that were set during the Civil War, as well as a lot of fighting scenes. "It's got action," Taylor Lautner confirmed to *Popstar!* magazine. "The action levels continue to build. In *Eclipse*, it's the three of them [Edward, Jacob, and Bella] actually physically together. And we have to team up and make this decision to try and be friends to protect

Bella. It's the ultimate high point of the story." With each movie getting bigger and better, it sounds like all of the exciting action in *Eclipse* will be sure to please fans!

Boo Boo was also excited about filming—in fact, he was so excited that he was now a part of the *Twilight* world that he couldn't wait to share it with fans! On September 24, Boo Boo posted a photo of himself in his Seth Clearwater costume on Twitter—with the sleeve of his T-shirt rolled up so that his "wolf pack" tattoo was showing! His fans must have gone wild with anticipation to finally see him in character!

After just over two months of shooting, on October 29, 2009, David Slade posted on Twitter that they had completed all of the principal photography for the film shoot. Principal photography is what the actual filming of the movie is called, which comes after the pre-production preparation beforehand, and is then followed by the post-production phase, which includes adding special effects, editing, adding the musical soundtrack, and so on. The director tweeted that he was: "Physically and emotionally exhausted."

And no wonder! Packing all of the excitement of *Eclipse* into two months of filming must have been challenging, but also very exciting and fun!

Luckily for Boo Boo, although his movie wouldn't be out for another seven months, he still got a little taste of what it was like to be a part of the *Twilight* phenomenon when he attended the red-carpet premiere of *The Twilight Saga: New Moon* on November 14, 2009, in Hollywood.

"You've never seen anything like it," he told the Ministry of Gossip blog for the *Los Angeles Times*. "The fans were screaming, it was awesome." And the attention didn't stop there. When Boo Boo and his date for the night, little sister Fivel, got their hair done at West Hollywood's Parlour on 3rd for the premiere, they were greeted by hordes of photographers desperate to snap pictures of the newest *Twilight* star! "The second we left the salon, there were paparazzi everywhere," Boo Boo told the blog.

In fact, *Twilight* fans had started lining up days before the premiere in hopes of getting even a glimpse of their favorite stars! Boo Boo had been invited to attend the premiere of *Planet 51*, an animated movie starring Dwayne "The Rock" Johnson as an astronaut who ends up on another planet, two days before *The Twilight Saga: New Moon* premiered at the same theater. And when he got to that premiere, he was greeted by *Twilight* fans who were screaming his name and asking for autographs!

"All I can say is it was awesome," Boo Boo told about.com. "It's a dream come true, you know? This Twilight Saga is incredible right now and it's so huge. People are camping out over there. It was awesome." Boo Boo must have been amazed at how quickly his life turned around, going from a working actor with some very loyal fans, to a well-known star with thousands of people screaming for his autograph! But he was probably somewhat prepared by seeing how popular his old pal Taylor had become after the first *Twilight* movie came out. Just another reason Boo Boo was lucky to have Taylor as a friend!

Boo Boo attended the premiere of *The Twilight Saga: New Moon* with his sister Fivel, and they must have had a great time! And he definitely loved the movie. He told the Ministry of Gossip blog: "It was really good. The fight scenes in there between the wolves [and the vampires] were so cool." And at the after party, he was excited to hang out with his *Eclipse* director David Slade.

It's definitely been a whirlwind for Boo Boo. Even though he has lived in Hollywood and been around movie sets his whole life, nothing could prepare him for the passion that *Twilight* fans feel for the actors and actresses that bring their beloved characters to life on the big screen. Boo Boo told Maximo TV: "It was just incredible, the experience, cast, crew, everyone was amazing, and I'm just having a great time. Every time I see a *Twilight* poster or something, it's . . . I'm like, 'Wow, I can't believe I'm a part of that!'" Nice to see that Boo Boo is so grateful for his good fortune.

And things are sure to get even bigger for the *Twilight* cast—literally! *Eclipse* will be the first of the *Twilight* movies to be screened in IMAX theaters, which will allow audiences a whole new way to see their favorite characters on-screen. One thing's for sure, the fans are certainly grateful that Boo Boo is now a part of the Twilight Saga!

CHAPTER 9

WHAT'S NEXT FOR BOO BOO?

Boo Boo has definitely kept himself busy with his career as an entertainer—and he's not about to slow down! In addition to *The Twilight Saga: Eclipse,* Boo Boo has been busy filming lots of other movies and TV shows. After he completed filming his *Eclipse* role, he moved on to guest star in the hit CBS procedural crime show *CSI: Miami,* a Florida-based spin-off series of the original Las Vegas team of crime scene investigators, a police unit that helps solve murders and other crimes through technology. Boo Boo tweeted about how he thought his role on the show was "so cool." Once he got on the set, he also tweeted about his experience there with the lead actor, David Caruso, who plays Lieutenant Horatio Caine on the show: "I'm having an awesome time, David Caruso is so nice." And he also mentioned that he loved the yummy food on the craft services table, too! Sounds like a good gig! The episode, "Die by the Sword," aired in January 2010 as part of the eighth season of the long-running drama.

Also, several movies that Boo Boo filmed before *The Twilight Saga: Eclipse* are making their way into theaters and video stores, including the dark comedy *American Cowslip*, the thriller *Dark Games*, the coming-of-age drama *Smitty*, and the comedy-drama *Logan*.

American Cowslip centers around Ethan, an eccentric poker player who is hiding a crippling addiction. He enters a Garden of the Year contest in hopes of winning $10,000. The movie stars such famous actors as Cloris Leachman and Val Kilmer, as well as Rip Torn, who plays the character Trevor in the movie. Boo Boo plays the role of Cary in the movie, and got to shoot most of his scenes with Rip. He told *Teen Scene* magazine, "I have been shooting with Rip Torn. He is funny."

"I play a punk kid in the movie," Boo Boo told kidzworld.com. "I wear leather, a whole outfit, and it was really hot out every day and I had a dripping shirt! And I ride this really cool bike 'cause I ride all around and it was really fun to do!"

After filming for *American Cowslip* wrapped, Boo Boo went to New Mexico to work on *Dark Games*, a thriller in which Boo Boo's character, Jake Wincott, witnesses a crime. *Dark Games* is another family affair, as Boo Boo's big sister, Maegan, has a role in the movie, too; she plays the role of Linda Morehouse. And Nils Sr. is involved in the film, too; he's the assistant director! Nils Sr. and Maegan also did stunt work for the film, and Boo Boo and his dad worked together to compose music for the soundtrack! "It's going to be really good!" Boo Boo told *Teen Scene* magazine.

After that, Boo Boo switched gears again to play the role of Peabo in *Smitty*, about a Chicago boy, Ben, played by Brandon Tyler Russell, who has to spend the summer with his grandfather on a farm after Peabo gets him in trouble with the cops. Boo Boo's talented costars include Academy Award–winning actress Mira Sorvino as Ben's mom and Peter Fonda as Ben's grandfather. "It's just a great cast, and I had a great time filming it," Boo Boo told *Popstar!* magazine. *Smitty* was directed by David M. Evans, who also wrote and directed the hilarious '90s family comedy *The Sandlot*. *The Sandlot* is about a boy named Scotty who moves to a new neighborhood in the 1960s, and learns to play baseball with his new friends.

The year 2010 will go down as a busy one for Boo Boo—in addition to *The Twilight Saga: Eclipse* and *Smitty,* his movie *Logan* will also be among the films in theaters. *Logan* is about two brothers, Logan and Tyler Hoffman, played by Leo Howard and Patrick Probst. Logan wants his brother to help him with a seemingly impossible project. Boo Boo plays the character of Ben in the movie, which was filmed in St. Louis, Missouri.

And after that? Well, there is definitely the possibility of more Seth Clearwater in the future! After all, there are four books in the *Twilight* series, so far, with *Breaking Dawn* as the fourth title in the saga. But when Boo Boo was asked about the future of the film series, it seems he might have made a bit of a boo-boo himself! "I heard there's going to be three more movies," Boo Boo told *Access Hollywood* in an interview. "*Eclipse, Breaking Dawn,* and there should be one more." Unfortunately, Boo Boo soon realized he might not have had all the details of the story straight.

"We appreciate our young actor's enthusiasm for the franchise and his role, but his comments about the number of films were unfortunately uninformed and not accurate," a Summit Entertainment representative told usmagazine.com after Boo Boo's *Access Hollywood* interview. "However, the fans should rest assured [that] we're working with Stephenie Meyer to bring *Breaking Dawn* to the big screen."

Boo Boo soon apologized for his mistake, telling radaronline.com, "There was some false communication, so far it's just *Eclipse* that's coming out." He was probably just so excited about playing Seth that he was hoping he'd get several more chances to play the character! And as popular as the Twilight Saga movies have all been so far, we'll just have to wait and see what happens!

CHAPTER 10
BOO BOO AND HIS FANS

Not only is Boo Boo a very talented actor, singer, dancer, and martial artist, but he also knows what's important to him—namely, his fans! Boo Boo owns a Gibson guitar, and he loves it so much that he signed an exclusive artist contract with Gibson Guitars, which means that when he's rocking out onstage with his band, he only uses a Gibson. And in January 2008, he decided to throw himself a birthday party at the Gibson showroom in Los Angeles. Not only that, but he invited all of his fans! What a great guy!

Gibson guitars have been beloved by musicians for years and years, dating all the way back to the 1930s! Many rock musicians have famously played Gibson guitars, including classic rockers like Eric Clapton, Sheryl Crow, Jimi Hendrix, Bob Dylan, Paul McCartney, Billie Joe Armstrong of Green Day, The Edge from U2, James Hetfield of Metallica,

Lenny Kravitz, Eddie Van Halen, and Slash from Guns N' Roses.

But Boo Boo also likes to have his fans help out good causes, too. He's known for donating his valuable time to charities like A Place Called Home, the Los Angeles Mission, Athletes and Entertainers for Kids, and the Make-A-Wish Foundation. And when *The Twilight Saga: New Moon* opened nationwide, Boo Boo decided to use his name to offer fans a chance to meet him, and help out yet another charity in the process!

LifeSource, the leading blood supply center in the Chicago, Illinois, area, decided to host a special blood drive event on October 24, 2009, with a *The Twilight Saga: New Moon* theme. Makes perfect sense, since vampires need blood to live! And when he was asked if he'd mind stopping by, Boo Boo happily agreed to make an appearance at the event. The first 250 donors who scheduled an appointment to donate blood at the blood drive received a free pair of tickets to a special midnight screening of *The Twilight Saga: New Moon* on November 19, 2009, the night before the movie's official opening day!

And the next 250 donors who registered received not only a free ticket to the midnight screening, but they also got a wristband to meet Boo Boo in person at the blood drive! And in addition, they got their very own signed photo of Boo Boo!

LifeSource knew that by combining forces with *Twilight* and Boo Boo, they would be able to reach out to even more people, which is an important thing for charities, since by definition they rely on the generosity and compassion of people. "By focusing on what is hot in pop culture, in this case the *Twilight* craze, we can engage a very important audience," said Judi Matok, vice president and chief operating officer of LifeSource. "Our goal is to make blood donation fun and educate younger audiences on the importance of giving back to the community. We also want to raise awareness that when people donate one pint of blood they can save up to three lives right here in the Chicago area." And boy, did it work! The event, combined with Boo Boo's appearance, helped LifeSource record the largest blood donation in the entire history of the company! Way to go, Boo Boo!

Giving blood must be a very important cause for Boo Boo—on December 12, 2009, he attended the BrittiCares International Foundation's 3rd Annual Blood Drive at the Childrens Hospital Los Angeles, and even brought along his parents and little sisters, Fivel and Sage. BrittiCares was founded in honor of a little girl named Brittiana Henderson who fought courageously against bone cancer and leukemia. Donating blood is an important way that people can help others who are sick. If you want to help out your community by donating blood, there are lots of ways to do it. Donors must be at least seventeen years old and in good health. You can learn more about donating blood by visiting the website of the American Red Cross at redcrossblood.org.

In addition to helping out those in need, Boo Boo also likes to bring his cool sense of style to his fans. In 2009, Graffeeti Shoes, the company that created the amazing new ReMARKable write-on sneaker, introduced their new Boo Boo Stewart line of "signature sneakers." The sneakers come with cool write-on panels and five colored dry-erase markers, so that Boo Boo's fans can customize their own sneakers however they'd like!

"I immediately clicked with the Graffeeti sneakers because I have always been a doodler," said Boo Boo in a press release. "I was like, wow, you can just wipe it off and keep doodling? I'm a Graffeeti natural for sure, and I also really like the company's commitment to giving back. [The owners of Graffeeti have committed to making annual contributions to children's charities, based on a percentage of their profits.] That's important to me. We're a perfect pair." In fact, there's even been talk that Boo Boo might help to develop even more products for Graffeeti. Visit the company's website, graffeeti.com, for more information on how to order your very own Boo Boo shoes!

And if wearing a pair of Boo Boo's shoes isn't enough for you, maybe you could be lucky enough to be the type of girl that Boo Boo likes to spend time with! Just be sure to have a big smile on your face! Boo Boo told *Popstar!* magazine that the first thing he notices when a girl walks into the room is "definitely her smile." Aw! But Boo Boo does acknowledge that he hasn't had much time to think about girlfriends lately. "I've been focusing on my career a lot," he confessed to *Popstar!* But even so, that doesn't mean you couldn't still be friends with him—Boo Boo "definitely" thinks that guys and girls can be just friends. "My sisters have a lot of guy friends that are just that," he told *Popstar!*

Boo Boo really does appreciate his fans and listens to them. After all, he might not have won the role of Seth in *The Twilight Saga: Eclipse* if it weren't for one of his loyal fans! So Boo Boo tries to keep in touch with his fans, because he wants them to feel like they are a part of his life and career, no matter where they live. What better way to do that than by posting things online for them?

Boo Boo and his sister Fivel both like to record lots of videos of each other, whether it's singing, performing martial arts tricks, or even just hanging out. Then they'll post them on YouTube on their TSC Promotions channel for their fans to watch. Boo Boo and his mother both Twitter, as well! Twitter is the free social networking and micro-blogging site, where users can post quick thoughts or "tweets"—but only up to 140 typed characters at a time! Renee posts at @mammarazzi1, where she keeps fans updated on what both Boo Boo and Fivel are up to—including posting lots of candid photos of the whole family on Twitpic, which is where Twitter users can easily post photos for their Twitter followers to see.

Boo Boo liked seeing what Renee was posting so much that he even went so far as to set up a separate, special Twitter account, @booboostewart, just so he could talk to his fans, and hear back from them! When they post nice tweets about him, Boo Boo will often thank them by mentioning their Twitter names in his tweets. And he sometimes holds contests where he'll "follow" the first three fans who send tweets to him, meaning he'll subscribe to their Twitter feeds! So if you have a Twitter account, who knows—Boo Boo could end up "following" you if you're lucky!

CHAPTER 11

FUN, FAST BOO BOO FACTS

FULL NAME: Nils Allen Stewart Jr.

DATE OF BIRTH: January 21, 1994

ZODIAC SIGN: Aquarius

HOMETOWN: Beverly Hills, California

CURRENT RESIDENCE: Shadow Hills, California

SIBLINGS: older sister: Maegan, younger sisters: Trent Heaven ("Fivel") and Sage

PARENTS: Nils Allen Stewart Sr. and Renee Stewart

HEIGHT: 5' 5"

HAIR COLOR: black

HOBBIES: karate, dance, singing, guitar, stunts, gymnastics, magic

FAVORITE FOODS: tiki masala (Indian food), chicken, waffles

FAVORITE HEALTHY FOODS: tofu and avocados (but not together!)

FAVORITE RESTAURANT: McDonald's

FAVORITE ICE CREAM FLAVORS: mint and chip

FAVORITE CANDY: sour candy

FAVORITE ACTORS: Mel Gibson and Heath Ledger

FAVORITE ACTRESS: Angelina Jolie

DREAM COSTAR: Tom Cruise

FAVORITE BOOKS: *Twilight* series, bio on Heath Ledger

FAVORITE MOVIES: *The Lord of the Rings* trilogy, *Mission: Impossible*, *The Wrestler*

FAVORITE TYPE OF MUSIC: rock

FAVORITE MUSICIANS: Guns N' Roses, Disturbed, Dave Navarro

FAVORITE COLOR: green

FAVORITE SPORT: karate

FAVORITE WRESTLER: Kane

FAVORITE PLACE TO TRAVEL: Europe

FAVORITE TYPE OF WEATHER: rainy days

FAVORITE THING TO DO: play guitar or drums

IF HE WEREN'T AN ENTERTAINER, HE'D LIKE TO BE: an animation artist. "I had the chance to meet with Stan Lee who gave me advice—he is amazing!" Boo Boo told *Inspire* magazine.

CHAPTER 12
HOW WELL DO YOU KNOW BOO BOO?

Now that you've had a chance to read up on all things Boo Boo, are you ready to find out just how well you know him? Take this fun quiz to test your Boo Boo IQ!

1) Boo Boo's hometown is:
   - **A.** Beverly Hills, California
   - **B.** Phoenix, Arizona
   - **C.** Seattle, Washington

2) Boo Boo and his father both appeared on what long-running television show?
   - **A.** *Law & Order*
   - **B.** *CSI: Crime Scene Investigation*
   - **C.** *ER*

3) How many Martial Arts World Championships has Boo Boo won?
   - **A.** One
   - **B.** Two
   - **C.** Three

4) What is Boo Boo's favorite color?

   A. Green

   B. Blue

   C. Black

5) What is Boo Boo's favorite fast-food restaurant?

   A. Taco Bell

   B. Burger King

   C. McDonald's

6) How old was Boo Boo when he first started to practice karate?

   A. Three

   B. Five

   C. Seven

7) Which of Boo Boo's sisters did he take with him to *The Twilight Saga: New Moon* movie premiere?

   A. Maegan

   B. Fivel

   C. Sage

8) Which successful musical artist or band has Boo Boo gone on tour with?

  A. Cheetah Girls

  B. Miley Cyrus

  C. Jonas Brothers

9) Which talk show hosted Boo Boo and the rest of the Sideswipe Kids for their first national television appearance?

  A. *Live with Regis & Kelly*

  B. *The Ellen DeGeneres Show*

  C. *The Oprah Winfrey Show*

10) Which movie villain did Boo Boo decide to dress up as for his Halloween costume in 2009?

  A. Voldemort

  B. The Green Goblin

  C. The Joker

11) What line of musical instruments does Boo Boo exclusively represent?

  A. Fender

  B. Gibson

  C. Yamaha

12) How tall is Boo Boo?

    A. 5' 2"

    B. 5' 5"

    C. 6' 3"

13) What CGI movie featured Boo Boo in a small role?

    A. *The Polar Express*

    B. *Beowulf*

    C. *Star Wars: The Clone Wars*

14) Boo Boo appeared in a sitcom based on the life of which famous stand-up comedian?

    A. Jerry Seinfeld

    B. Roseanne

    C. Chris Rock

15) Boo Boo was the host of what syndicated news program for kids?

    A. *Blue Dolphin Kids*

    B. *Green Cove*

    C. *The Wolf Pack*

16) Which successful pop musician did *not* get their start with Walt Disney, like Boo Boo did?

A. Christina Aguilera

B. Miley Cyrus

C. Justin Bieber

17) What did Boo Boo love to have as part of his *Eclipse* training diet?

A. Muscle Milk

B. Clif Bars

C. Cheerios

18) Which member of the *Twilight* cast did Boo Boo already know before he got the part of Seth?

A. Kristen Stewart

B. Robert Pattinson

C. Taylor Lautner

19) Who directed Boo Boo in *Eclipse*?

A. Catherine Hardwicke

B. Chris Weitz

C. David Slade

20) What kind of day does Boo Boo like the most?

A. Sunny

B. Rainy

C. Snowy

ANSWERS: 1. A, 2. C, 3. B, 4. A, 5. C, 6. A, 7. B, 8. A, B, or C, 9. B, 10. C, 11. B, 12. B, 13. B, 14. C, 15. A, 16. C, 17. A, 18. C, 19. C, 20. B

If you answered less than ten questions correctly, you are a Boo Boo admirer. You've only recently gotten to know about Boo Boo Stewart, and you're learning all about him and his different projects and accomplishments. But if you keep reading up on him, you'll soon know Boo Boo like the back of your hand!

If you answered ten to fifteen questions correctly, you are a solid Boo Boo fan. You've watched him in movies and on TV, and have probably even downloaded a few of his songs. You love to find out new information about him, and are starting to commit even some of the more obscure bits of Boo Boo trivia to memory. You've probably already asked your friends which of them wants to see *The Twilight Saga: Eclipse* with you. And the more you get to know about Boo Boo, the more you love him!

If you answered more than fifteen questions correctly, you are a big-time Boo Boo fanatic! When it comes to all things Boo Boo, you're the resident expert. You're first in line for his movies, and own all of his songs. Your walls are probably covered with posters of Boo Boo, and you might even have a screen saver of him on your computer! Boo Boo can be sure that you'll be following his every move, and he's super-appreciative of dedicated fans like you!

CHAPTER 13
WHAT KIND OF BOO BOO FAN ARE YOU?

Boo Boo is one of the most talented teen performers around—he sings, dances, and plays guitar and drums; he's a martial arts champion; and he's one of the hottest rising actors on the Hollywood scene! You might be a big fan of Boo Boo's, but what side of Boo Boo appeals to you the most? Which Boo Boo would you want to spend the day with? Take this quiz and find out which part of Boo Boo you're most compatible with!

1) It's your birthday, and you've got a stack of great gift cards in your hand. Where would you head first to start shopping?

   A. Log on to your computer to download some great new songs from iTunes or Amazon!

   B. Sign up for a Netflix account and start queuing up some great videos to rent!

C. Head to Foot Locker for that new pair of running shoes you've had your eye on!

2) If you had to pick a theme song to best represent yourself, what would it be?

    A. "Fame" by Naturi Naughton

    B. "Beverly Hills" by Weezer

    C. "Kung Fu Fighting" by Cee-Lo & Jack Black

3) It's the first day of summer vacation—how do you want to spend the day?

    A. Get together with some friends for a karaoke party!

    B. Stay inside and catch up on some movies on HBO!

    C. Head out for a run to get some exercise!

4) You're at a party with Boo Boo, and he offers to introduce you to one of his friends. Who would you want to meet the most?

A. Miley Cyrus would be awesome!

B. Taylor Lautner! Are you kidding?!?

C. Wait, is that really Mike Chat, a real-life Power Ranger?

If you chose . . .

Mostly As—You're a rocker at heart! You love music almost as much as Boo Boo does! With Boo Boo on the guitar, and you rocking the mic, the two of you could make some great music, we're sure!

Mostly Bs—You're a total fan of the silver screen, and Boo Boo's acting career is what's most appealing to you! You love the glitz and the glamour of show business, and the land of make-believe that is Hollywood! Sunset Strip, here you come!

Mostly Cs—Boo Boo's martial arts mastery is where it's at for you! You enjoy being athletic and energetic, and staying in shape is important to you. Boo Boo would make a great workout partner at the gym!

CHAPTER 14
BOO BOO ONLINE

Boo Boo Stewart is a triple threat: an actor, singer, and martial artist who is always keeping the entertainment news media abuzz with his latest projects. Weekly magazines, newspapers, websites, and blogs all run stories about what Boo Boo is up to next. But Boo Boo is also really good about telling his fans what he's been doing online, so it's super easy to get your next Boo Boo fix!

But always be careful online, and never give out any sort of personal information—like your name, address, or phone number, or even the name of your school or sports team—and never try to meet someone in person that you only know from the Internet.

Also, when you surf the Net, remember that not everything you read online is true. There are lots of people out there creating websites, and some of them might occasionally post false information, just to make their website seem more exciting. So always take what you read online with a grain of salt. And remember, you should never surf the Web without your parents' permission.

If you can't find your favorite Boo Boo website next time you log on, don't worry about it—websites come and go. There will be another Boo Boo fansite popping up soon enough to replace it!

www.imdb.com/name/nm1559927

The Internet Movie Database (or IMDB) is a great place to keep track of what projects actors like Boo Boo have completed. It has helpful information like who else is starring in Boo Boo's latest movie, as well as release dates and links to official websites.

www.twitter.com/mammarazzi1

Boo Boo and Fivel both post updates on this Twitter account—it belongs to their mom, Renee Stewart! (Boo Boo and Fivel both tease their mom and call her MammaRazzi, like paparazzi, because she's always taking pictures of them!)

www.twitter.com/booboostewart

Boo Boo also has a separate Twitter account just to talk with his fans! (What a great guy!) If you're lucky, he just might "follow" your account back!

www.myspace.com/booboosofficialfanclub

Boo Boo has several different MySpace pages set up for his musical projects, including ones for T-Squad, Echoes of Angels, and his own solo music projects. There's also an official fan club page on MySpace.

www.facebook.com/pages/Boo-Boo-Stewart/153447247787

Facebook also has some Boo Boo fan pages and groups, including this one. Boo Boo isn't involved, but fans can post news and links to other stories they've read about Boo Boo.

www.youtube.com/ren4165

Boo Boo also has his own account on YouTube, where he'll post videos of himself and his sisters.

www.teambooboo.com

Team Boo Boo is a fan site that Boo Boo supports—in fact, on his Twitter page, he tells people to visit Team Boo Boo for all the latest news!

www.myspace.com/booboostewartmusic
www.myspace.com/disneysnewgrouptsquad
www.myspace.com/tsquadmusicfansite
www.myspace.com/tsc_juvenile